A
Traveller In
War-Time

Winston Churchill

1st WORLD
LIBRARY
Literary Society

A Traveller In War-Time

Winston Churchill

© 1st World Library – Literary Society, 2004
PO Box 2211
Fairfield, IA 52556
www.1stworldlibrary.org
First Edition

LCCN: 2003099806

ISBN: 1-59540-130-X

Purchase *"A Traveller In War-Time"*
as a traditional bound book at:
www.1stWorldLibrary.org/purchase.asp?ISBN= 1-59540-130-X

1st World Library Literary Society is a nonprofit organization dedicated to promoting literacy by:

- Creating a free internet library accessible from any computer worldwide.
- Hosting writing competitions and offering book publishing scholarships.

Readers interested in supporting literacy
through sponsorship, donations or
membership please contact:
literacy@1stworldlibrary.org
Check us out at: www.1stworldlibrary.org

A Traveller In War-Time

contributed by Ed, Tim & Rodney
in support of
1st World Library Literary Society

PREFACE

I am reprinting here, in response to requests, certain recent experiences in Great Britain and France. These were selected in the hope of conveying to American readers some idea of the atmosphere, of "what it is like" in these countries under the immediate shadow of the battle clouds. It was what I myself most wished to know. My idea was first to send home my impressions while they were fresh, and to refrain as far as possible from comment and judgment until I should have had time to make a fuller survey. Hence I chose as a title for these articles, - intended to be preliminary," A Traveller in War-Time." I tried to banish from my mind all previous impressions gained from reading. I wished to be free for the moment to accept and record the chance invitation or adventure, wherever met with, at the Front, in the streets of Paris, in Ireland, or on the London omnibus. Later on, I hoped to write a book summarizing the changing social conditions as I had found them.

Unfortunately for me, my stay was unexpectedly cut short. I was able to avail myself of but few of the many opportunities offered. With this apology, the articles are presented as they were written.

I have given the impression that at the time of my visit there was no lack of food in England, but I fear that I have not done justice to the frugality of the people, much of which was self-imposed for the purpose of helping to win the war. On very, good authority I have been given to understand that food was less abundant during the winter just past; partly because of the effect of the severe weather on our American railroads, which had trouble in getting supplies to the coast, and partly because more and more ships were required for transporting American troops and supplies for these troops, to France. This additional curtailment was most felt by families of small income, whose earners were at the front or away on other government service. Mothers had great difficulty in getting adequate nourishment for growing children. But the British people cheerfully submitted to this further deprivation. Summer is at hand. It is to be hoped that before another winter sets in, American and British shipping will have sufficiently increased to remedy the situation.

In regard to what I have said of the British army, I was profoundly struck, as were other visitors to that front, by the health and morale of the men, by the marvel of organization accomplished in so comparatively brief a time. It was one of the many proofs of the extent to which the British nation had been socialized. When one thought of that little band of regulars sent to France in 1914, who became immortal at Mons, who shared the glory of the Marne, and in that first dreadful winter held back the German hosts from the Channel ports, the presence on the battle line of millions of disciplined and determined men seemed astonishing indeed. And this had been accomplished by a nation facing the gravest crisis in its history, under the necessity of sustaining and financing many allies and of protecting an Empire. Since my return to America a serious reverse has occurred.

After the Russian peace, the Germans attempted to overwhelm the British by hurling against them vastly superior numbers of highly trained men. It is for the military critic of the future to analyse any tactical errors that may have been made at the second battle of the Somme. Apparently there was an absence of preparation, of specific orders from high sources in the event of having to cede ground. This much can be said, that the morale of the British Army remains unimpaired; that the presence of mind and ability of the great majority of the officers who, flung on their own resources, conducted the retreat, cannot be questioned; while the accomplishment of General Carey, in stopping the gap with an improvised force of non-combatants, will go down in history. In an attempt to bring home to myself, as well as to my readers, a realization of what American participation in this war means or should mean.

CHAPTER I

Toward the end of the summer of 1917 it was very hot in New York, and hotter still aboard the transatlantic liner thrust between the piers. One glance at our cabins, at the crowded decks and diningroom, at the little writing-room above, where the ink had congealed in the ink-wells, sufficed to bring home to us that the days of luxurious sea travel, of a la carte restaurants, and Louis Seize bedrooms were gone - at least for a period. The prospect of a voyage of nearly two weeks was not enticing. The ship, to be sure, was far from being the best of those still running on a line which had gained a magic reputation of immunity from submarines; three years ago she carried only second and third class passengers! But most of us were in a hurry to get to the countries where war had already become a grim and terrible reality. In one way or another we had all enlisted.

By "we" I mean the American passengers. The first welcome discovery among the crowd wandering aimlessly and somewhat disconsolately about the decks was the cheerful face of a friend whom at first I did not recognize because of his amazing disguise in uniform. Hitherto he had been associated in my mind with dinner parties and clubs.

That life was past. He had laid up his yacht and joined

Winston Churchill

the Red Cross and, henceforth, for an indeterminable period, he was to abide amidst the discomforts and dangers of the Western Front, with five days' leave every three months. The members of a group similarly attired whom I found gathered by the after-rail were likewise cheerful. Two well-known specialists from the Massachusetts General Hospital made significant the hegira now taking place that threatens to leave our country, like Britain, almost doctorless. When I reached France it seemed to me that I met all the celebrated medical men I ever heard of. A third in the group was a business man from the Middle West who had wound up his affairs and left a startled family in charge of a trust company. Though his physical activities had hitherto consisted of an occasional mild game of golf, he wore his khaki like an old campaigner; and he seemed undaunted by the prospect - still somewhat remotely ahead of him - of a winter journey across the Albanian Mountains from the Aegean to the Adriatic.

After a restless night, we sailed away in the hot dawn of a Wednesday. The shores of America faded behind us, and as the days went by, we had the odd sense of threading uncharted seas; we found it more and more difficult to believe that this empty, lonesome ocean was the Atlantic in the twentieth century. Once we saw a four-master; once a shy, silent steamer avoided us, westward bound; and once in mid-ocean, tossed on a sea sun-silvered under a rack of clouds, we overtook a gallant little schooner out of New Bedford or Gloucester - a forthfarer, too.

Meanwhile, amongst the Americans, the socializing process had begun.

Many elements which in a former stratified existence would never have been brought into contact were fusing by the pressure of a purpose, of a great adventure common to us all. On the upper deck, high above the waves, was a little 'fumoir' which, by some odd trick of association, reminded me of the villa formerly occupied by the Kaiser in Corfu - perhaps because of the faience plaques set in the walls - although I cannot now recall whether the villa has faience plaques or not. The room was, of course, on the order of a French provincial cafe, and as such delighted the bourgeoisie monopolizing the alcove tables and joking with the fat steward. Here in this 'fumoir', lawyers, doctors, business men of all descriptions, newspaper correspondents, movie photographers, and millionaires who had never crossed save in a 'cabine de luxe', rubbed elbows and exchanged views and played bridge together. There were Y. M. C. A. people on their way to the various camps, reconstruction workers intending to build temporary homes for the homeless French, and youngsters in the uniform of the American Field Service, going over to drive camions and ambulances; many of whom, without undue regret, had left college after a freshman year. They invaded the 'fumoir', undaunted, to practise atrocious French on the phlegmatic steward; they took possession of a protesting piano in the banal little salon and sang: "We'll not come back till it's over over there." And in the evening, on the darkened decks, we listened and thrilled to the refrain:

"There's a long, long trail a-winding
Into the land of my dreams."

We were Argonauts - even the Red Cross ladies on

their way to establish rest camps behind the lines and brave the mud and rains of a winter in eastern France. None, indeed, were more imbued with the forthfaring spirit than these women, who were leaving, without regret, sheltered, comfortable lives to face hardships and brave dangers without a question. And no sharper proof of the failure of the old social order to provide for human instincts and needs could be found than the conviction they gave of new and vitalizing forces released in them. The timidities with which their sex is supposedly encumbered had disappeared, and even the possibility of a disaster at sea held no terrors for them. When the sun fell down into the warm waters of the Gulf Stream and the cabins below were sealed - and thus become insupportable - they settled themselves for the night in their steamer-chairs and smiled at the remark of M. le Commissaire that it was a good "season" for submarines. The moonlight filtered through the chinks in the burlap shrouding the deck. About 3 a.m. the khaki-clad lawyer from Milwaukee became communicative, the Red Cross ladies produced chocolate. It was the genial hour before the final nap, from which one awoke abruptly at the sound of squeegees and brooms to find the deck a river of sea water, on whose banks a wild scramble for slippers and biscuit-boxes invariably ensued. No experience could have been more socializing.

"Well, it's a relief," one of the ladies exclaimed, "not to be travelling with half a dozen trunks and a hat-box! Oh, yes, I realize what I'm doing. I'm going to live in one of those flimsy portable houses with twenty cots and no privacy and wear the same clothes for months, but it's better than thrashing around looking for something to do and never finding it, never getting anything real to spend one's energy-on. I've closed my country house, I've sublet my apartment, I've done with teas and bridge, and I'm happier than I've been in my life even if I don't get enough sleep."

Another lady, who looked still young, had two sons in the army. "There was nothing for me to do but sit around the house and wait, and I want to be useful. My husband has to stay at home; he can't leave his business." Be useful! There she struck the new and aggressive note of emancipation from the restricted self-sacrifice of the old order, of wider service for the unnamed and the unknown; and, above all, for the wider self-realization of which service is but a by-product. I recall particularly among these women a young widow with an eager look in clear grey eyes that gazed eastward into the unknown with hope renewed. Had she lived a quarter of a century ago she might have been doomed to slow desiccation. There are thousands of such women in France today, and to them the great war has brought salvation.

From what country other than America could so many thousands of pilgrims - even before our nation had entered the war - have hurried across a wide ocean to take their part? No matter what religion we profess, whether it be Calvinism, or Catholicism, we are individualists, pragmatists, empiricists for ever. Our faces are set toward strange worlds presently to rise out of the sea and take on form and colour and substance – worlds of new aspirations, of new ideas and new values. And on this voyage I was reminded of Josiah Royce's splendid summary of the American philosophy - of the American religion as set forth by William James:

"The spirit of the frontiers-man, of the gold-seeker

or the home-builder transferred to the meta-physical or to the religious realm. There is a far-off home, our long lost spiritual fortune. Experience alone can guide us to the place where these things are, hence indeed you need experience. You can only win your way on the frontier unless you are willing to live there."

Through the pall of horror and tragedy the American sees a vision; for him it is not merely a material and bloody contest of arms and men, a military victory to be gained over an aggressive and wrong-minded people. It is a world calamity, indeed, but a calamity, since it has come, to be spiritualized and utilized for the benefit of the future society of mankind. It must be made to serve a purpose in helping to liberate the world from sentimentalism, ignorance, close-mindedness, and cant.

II

One night we entered the danger zone. There had been an entertainment in the little salon which, packed with passengers, had gradually achieved the temperature and humidity of a Turkish bath. For the ports had been closed as tight as gaskets could make them, the electric fans, as usual, obstinately "refused to march." After the amateur speechmaking and concert pieces an Italian violinist, who had thrown over a lucrative contract to become a soldier, played exquisitely; and one of the French sisters we had seen walking the deck with the mincing steps of the cloister sang; somewhat precariously and pathetically, the Ave Maria. Its pathos was of the past, and after she had finished, as we fled into the open air, we were conscious of having turned our backs irrevocably yet determinedly upon an era whose life and convictions the music of the composer so beautifully expressed. And the sister's sweet withered face was reminiscent of a missal, one bright with colour, and still shining faintly. A missal in a library of modern books!

On deck a fine rain was blowing through a gap in our burlap shroud, a phosphorescent fringe of foam hissed along the sides of the ship, giving the illusory appearance of our deadlights open and ablaze, exaggerating the sinister blackness of the night. We were, apparently, a beacon in that sepia waste where modern undersea monsters were lurking.

There were on board other elements which in the normal times gone by would have seemed disquieting enough. The evening after we had left New York, while we were still off the coast of Long Island, I saw on the poop a crowd of steerage passengers listening intently to harangues by speakers addressing them from the top of a pile of life rafts. Armenians, I was told, on their way to fight the Turks, all recruited in America by one frenzied woman who had seen her child cut in two by a German officer. Twilight was gathering as I joined the group, the sea was silvered by the light of an August moon floating serenely between swaying stays. The orator's passionate words and gestures evoked wild responses from his hearers, whom the drag of an ancient hatred had snatched from the peaceful asylum of the west. This smiling, happy folk, which I had seen in our manufacturing towns and cities, were now transformed, atavistic - all save one, a student, who stared wistfully through his spectacles across the waters. Later, when twilight deepened, when the moon had changed from silver to gold, the orators gave place to a singer. He had been a bootblack in America. Now he had become a bard. His plaintive minor chant evoked, one knew not how, the flavour of that age-long history of oppression and wrong these were now determined to avenge. Their conventional costumes were proof that we had harboured them - almost, indeed, assimilated them. And suddenly they had reverted. They were going to slaughter the Turks.

On a bright Saturday afternoon we steamed into the wide mouth of the Gironde, a name stirring vague memories of romance and terror. The French passengers gazed wistfully at the low-lying strip of sand and forest, but our uniformed pilgrims crowded the rail and hailed it as the promised land of self-realization. A richly coloured watering-place slid into view, as in a moving-picture show. There was, indeed, all the reality and unreality of the cinematograph about our arrival; presently the reel would end abruptly, and we should find ourselves pushing our way out of the emptying theatre into a rainy street. The impression of unreality in the face of visual evidence persisted into the night when, after an afternoon at anchor, we glided up the river, our decks and ports ablaze across the land. Silhouettes of tall poplars loomed against the blackness; occasionally a lamp revealed the milky blue facade of a house. This was France! War-torn France - at last vividly brought home to us when a glare appeared on the sky, growing brighter and brighter until, at a turn of the river, abruptly we came abreast of vomiting furnaces, thousands of electric lights strung like beads over the crest of a hill, and, below these, dim rows of houses, all of a sameness, stretching along monotonous streets. A munitions town in the night.

One could have tossed a biscuit on the stone wharfs where the workmen, crouching over their tasks, straightened up at sight of us and cheered. And one cried out hoarsely, "Vous venez nous sauver, vous Americains" - "You come to save us" - an exclamation I was to hear again in the days that followed.

III

All day long, as the 'rapide' hurried us through the smiling wine country and past the well-remembered chateaux of the Loire, we wondered how we should find Paris - beautiful Paris, saved from violation as by a miracle! Our first discovery, after we had pushed our way out of the dim station into the obscurity of the street, was that of the absence of taxicabs. The horsedrawn buses ranged along the curb were reserved for the foresighted and privileged few. Men and women were rushing desperately about in search of conveyances, and in the midst of this confusion, undismayed, debonnair, I spied a rugged, slouch-hatted figure standing under a lamp - the unmistakable American soldier.

"Aren't there any cabs in Paris?" I asked.

"Oh, yes, they tell me they're here," he said. "I've given a man a dollar to chase one."

Evidently one of our millionaire privates who have aroused such burnings in the heart of the French poilu, with his five sous a day! We left him there, and staggered across the Seine with our bags. A French officer approached us. "You come from America," he said. "Let me help you." There was just enough light in the streets to prevent us from getting utterly lost, and we recognized the dark mass of the Tuileries as we crossed the gardens. The hotel we sought was still there, and its menu, save for the war-bread and the tiny portion of sugar, as irreproachable as ever.

The next morning, as if by magic, hundreds of taxis had sprung into existence, though they were much in demand. And in spite of the soldiers thronging the sunlit streets, Paris was seemingly the same Paris one had always known, gay - insouciante, pleasure-bent. The luxury shops appeared to be thriving, the world-renowned restaurants to be doing business as usual; to judge from the prices, a little better than usual; the expensive hotels were full. It is not the real France, of course, yet it seemed none the less surprising that it should still exist. Oddly enough the presence of such overwhelming numbers of soldiers should have failed to strike the note of war, emphasized that of lavishness, of the casting off of mundane troubles for which the French capital has so long been known. But so it was. Most of these soldiers were here precisely with the object of banishing from their minds the degradations and horrors of the region from which they had come, and which was so unbelievably near; a few hours in an automobile - less than that in one of those dragon-fly machines we saw intermittently hovering in the blue above our heads!

Paris, to most Americans, means that concentrated little district de luxe of which the Place Vendome is the centre, and we had always unconsciously thought of it as in the possession of the Anglo-Saxons. So it seems today. One saw hundreds of French soldiers, of course, in all sorts of uniforms, from the new grey blue and visor to the traditional cloth blouse and kepi; once in a while a smart French officer. The English and Canadians, the Australians, New Zealanders, and Americans were much in evidence. Set them down anywhere on the face of the globe, under any conditions conceivable, and you could not surprise them; such was the impression. The British officers and even the British Tommies were blase, wearing the air of the 'semaine Anglaise', and the "five o'clock tea," as the French delight to call it. That these could have come direct from the purgatory of the trenches seemed unbelievable. The Anzacs, with looped-up hats, strolled about, enjoying themselves, halting before the shops in the Rue de la Paix to gaze at the priceless jewellery there, or stopping at a sidewalk cafe to enjoy a drink. Our soldiers had not seen the front; many of them, no doubt, were on leave from the training-camps, others were on duty in Paris, but all seemed in a hurry to get somewhere, bound for a definite destination. They might have been in New York or San Francisco. It was a novel sight, indeed, to observe them striding across the Place Vendome with out so much as deigning to cast a glance at the column dedicated to the great emperor who fought that other world-war a century ago; to see our square-shouldered officers hustling around corners in Ford and Packard automobiles. And the atmosphere of our communication headquarters was so essentially one of "getting things done" as to make one forget the mediaeval narrowness of the Rue Sainte Anne, and the inconvenient French private-dwelling arrangements of the house. You were transported back to America. Such, too, was the air of our Red Cross establishment in the ancient building facing the Palace de la Concorde, where the unfortunate Louis lost his head.

History had been thrust into the background. I was never more aware of this than when, shortly after dawn Wednesday, the massive grey pile of the Palace of Versailles suddenly rose before me. As the motor shot through the empty Place d'Armes I made a desperate attempt to summon again a vivid impression, when I had first stood there many years ago, of an angry Paris mob beating against that grill, of the Swiss guards dying on the stairway for their Queen. But it was no use. France has undergone some subtle change, yet I knew I was in France. I knew it when we left Paris and sped through the dim leafy tunnels of the Bois; when I beheld a touch of filtered sunlight on the dense blue thatch of the 'marroniers' behind the walls of a vast estate once dedicated to the sports and pleasures of Kings; when I caught glimpses of silent chateaux mirrored in still waters.

I was on my way, with one of our naval officers, to visit an American naval base on the western coast. It was France, but the laughter had died on her lips. A few women and old men and children were to be seen in the villages, a bent figure in a field, an occasional cart that drew aside as we hurried at eighty kilometers an hour along deserted routes drawn as with a ruler across the land. Sometimes the road dipped into a canyon of poplars, and the sky between their crests was a tiny strip of mottled blue and white. The sun crept in and out, the clouds cast shadows on the hills; here and there the tower of lonely church or castle broke the line of a distant ridge. Morning-glories nodded over lodge walls where the ivy was turning crimson, and the little gardens were masses of colours - French colours like that in the beds of the Tuileries, brick-red geraniums and dahlias, yellow marigolds and purple asters.

We lunched at one of the little inns that for generations have been tucked away in the narrow streets of provincial towns; this time a Cheval Blanc, with an unimposing front and a blaze of sunshine in its heart. After a dejeuner fit for the most exacting of bon viveurs we sat in that courtyard and smoked, while an ancient waiter served us with coffee that dripped through silver percolators into our glasses. The tourists have fled. "If happily you should come again, monsieur," said madame, as she led me with pardonable pride through her immaculate bedrooms and salons with wavy floors. And I dwelt upon a future holiday there, on the joys of sharing with a friend that historic place. The next afternoon I lingered in another town, built on a little hill ringed about with ancient walls, from whose battlements tide-veined marshes stretched away to a gleaming sea. A figure flitting through the cobbled streets, a woman in black who sat sewing, sewing in a window, only served to heighten the impression of emptiness, to give birth to the odd fancy that some alchemic quality in the honeyed sunlight now steeping it must have preserved the place through the ages. But in the white close surrounding the church were signs that life still persisted. A peasant was drawing water at the pump, and the handle made a noise; a priest chatted with three French ladies who had come over from a neighbouring seaside resort. And then a woman in deep mourning emerged from a tiny shop and took her bicycle from against the wall and spoke to me.

"Vous etes Americain, monsieur?"

I acknowledged it.

"Vous venez nous sauver" - the same question I had heard on the lips of the workman in the night. "I hope so, madame," I replied, and would have added, "We come also to save ourselves." She looked at me with sad, questioning eyes, and I knew that for her - and alas for many like her - we were too late. When she had mounted her wheel and ridden away I bought a

'Matin' and sat down on a doorstep to read about Kerensky and the Russian Revolution. The thing seemed incredible here - war seemed incredible, and yet its tentacles had reached out to this peaceful Old World spot and taken a heavy toll. Once more I sought the ramparts, only to be reminded by those crumbling, machicolated ruins that I was in a war-ridden land. Few generations had escaped the pestilence.

At no great distance lay the little city which had been handed over to us by the French Government for a naval base, one of the ports where our troops and supplies are landed. Those who know provincial France will visualize its narrow streets and reticent shops, its grey-white and ecru houses all more or less of the same design, with long French windows guarded by ornamental balconies of cast iron - a city that has never experienced such a thing as a real-estate boom. Imagine, against such a background, the bewildering effect of the dynamic presence of a few regiments of our new army! It is a curious commentary on this war that one does not think of these young men as soldiers, but as citizens engaged in a scientific undertaking of a magnitude unprecedented. You come unexpectedly upon truck-loads of tanned youngsters, whose features, despite flannel shirts and campaign hats, summon up memories of Harvard Square and the Yale Yard, of campuses at Berkeley and Ithaca. The youthful drivers of these camions are alert, intent, but a hard day's work on the docks by no means suffices to dampen the spirits of the passengers, who whistle ragtime airs as they bump over the cobbles. And the note they strike is presently sustained by a glimpse, on a siding, of an efficient-looking Baldwin, ranged alongside several of the tiny French locomotives of yesterday; sustained, too, by an acquaintance with the young colonel in command of the town. Though an officer of the regular army, he brings home to one the fact that the days of the military martinet have gone for ever. He is military, indeed-erect and soldierly - but fortune has amazingly made him a mayor and an autocrat, a builder, and in some sense a railway-manager and superintendent of docks. And to these functions have been added those of police commissioner, of administrator of social welfare and hygiene. It will be a comfort to those at home to learn that their sons in our army in France are cared for as no enlisted men have ever been cared for before.

IV

By the end of September I had reached England, eager to gain a fresh impression of conditions there.

The weather in London was mild and clear. The third evening after I had got settled in one of those delightfully English hotels in the heart of the city, yet removed from the traffic, with letter-boxes that still bear the initials of Victoria, I went to visit some American naval officers in their sitting-room on the ground floor. The cloth had not been removed from the dinner-table, around which we were chatting, when a certain strange sound reached our ears - a sound not to be identified with the distant roar of the motor-busses in Pall Mall, nor with the sharp bark of the taxi-horns, although not unlike them. We sat listening intently, and heard the sound again.

"The Germans have come," one of the officers remarked, as he finished his coffee. The other looked at his watch. It was nine o'clock. "They must have left their lines about seven," he said.

In spite of the fact that our newspapers at home had made me familiar with these aeroplane raids, as I sat there, amidst those comfortable surroundings, the thing seemed absolutely incredible. To fly one hundred and fifty miles across the Channel and southern England, bomb London, and fly back again by midnight! We were going to be bombed! The anti-aircraft guns were already searching the sky for the invaders. It is sinister, and yet you are seized by an overwhelming curiosity that draws you, first to pull aside the heavy curtains of the window, and then to rush out into the dark street both proceedings in the worst possible form! The little street was deserted, but in Pall Mall the dark forms of busses could be made out scurrying for shelter, one wondered where? Above the roar of London, the pop pop pop! of the defending guns could be heard now almost continuously, followed by the shrieks and moans of the shrapnel shells as they passed close overhead. They sounded like giant rockets, and even as rockets some of them broke into a cascade of sparks. Star shells they are called, bursting, it seemed, among the immutable stars themselves that burned serenely on. And there were other stars like November meteors hurrying across space - the lights of the British planes scouring the heavens for their relentless enemies. Everywhere the restless white rays of the searchlights pierced the darkness, seeking, but seeking in vain. Not a sign of the intruders was to be seen. I was induced to return to the sitting-room.

"But what are they shooting at?" I asked.

"Listen," said one of the officers. There came a lull in the firing and then a faint, droning noise like the humming of insects on a still summer day. "It's all they have to shoot at, that noise."

"But their own planes?" I objected.

"The Gotha has two engines, it has a slightly different noise, when you get used to it. You'd better step out of that window. It's against the law to show light, and if a bomb falls in the street you'd be filled with glass." I overcame my fascination and obeyed. "It isn't only the bombs," my friend went on, "it's the falling shrapnel, too."

The noise made by those bombs is unmistakable, unforgetable, and quite distinct from the chorus of the guns and shrapnel - a crashing note, reverberating, sustained, like the E minor of some giant calliope.

In face of the raids, which coincide with the coming of the moon, London is calm, but naturally indignant over such methods of warfare. The damage done is ridiculously small; the percentage of deaths and injuries insignificant. There exists, in every large city, a riffraff to get panicky: these are mostly foreigners; they seek the Tubes, and some the crypt of St. Paul's, for it is wise to get under shelter during the brief period of the raids, and most citizens obey the warnings of the police. It is odd, indeed, that more people are not hurt by shrapnel. The Friday following the raid I have described I went out of town for a week-end, and returned on Tuesday to be informed that a shell had gone through the roof outside of the room I had vacated, and the ceiling and floor of the bedroom of one of the officers who lived below. He was covered with dust and debris, his lights went out, but he calmly stepped through the window. "You'd best have your dinner early, sir," I was told by the waiter on my return. "Last night a lady had her soup up-stairs, her chicken in the office, and her coffee in the cellar." It is worth while noting that she had all three. Another evening, when I was dining with Sir James Barrie, he showed me a handful of shrapnel fragments. "I gathered them off the roof," he informed me. And a lady next to whom I sat at luncheon told me in a matter-of-fact tone that a bomb had fallen the night before in the garden of her town house. "It was quite disagreeable," she said, "and broke all our windows on that side." During the last raids before the moon disappeared, by a new and ingenious system of barrage fire the Germans were driven off. The question of the ethics of reprisals is agitating London.

One "raid," which occurred at midday, is worth recording. I was on my way to our Embassy when, in the residential quarter through which I passed, I found all the housemaids in the areas gazing up at the sky, and I was told by a man in a grocer's cart that the Huns had come again. But the invader on this occasion turned out to be a British aviator from one of the camps who was bringing a message to London. The warmth of his reception was all that could be desired, and he alighted hastily in the first open space that presented itself.

Looking back to the time when I left America, I can recall the expectation of finding a Britain beginning to show signs of distress. I was prepared to live on a small ration. And the impression of the scarcity of food was seemingly confirmed when the table was being set for the first meal at my hotel; when the waiter, who chanced to be an old friend, pointed to a little bowl half-full of sugar and exclaimed: "I ought to warn you, sir, it's all you're to have for a week, and I'm sorry to say you're only allowed a bit of bread, too." It is human perversity to want a great deal of bread when bread becomes scarce; even war bread, which, by the way, is better than white. But the rest of the luncheon, when it came, proved that John Bull was under no necessity of stinting himself. Save for wheat and sugar; he is not in want. Everywhere in London you are confronted by signs of an incomprehensible prosperity; everywhere, indeed, in Great Britain. There can be no doubt about that of the wage-earners - nothing like it has ever been seen before. One sure sign of this is the phenomenal sale of pianos to households whose occupants had never dreamed of such luxuries. And not once, but many times, have I read in the newspapers of workingmen's families of four or five which are gaining collectively more than five hundred pounds a year. The economic and social significance of this tendency, the new attitude of the working classes, the ferment it is causing need not be dwelt upon here. That England will be a changed England is unquestionable.

The London theatres are full, the "movies" crowded, and you have to wait your turn for a seat at a restaurant. Bond Street and Piccadilly are doing a thriving business - never so thriving, you are told, and presently you are willing to believe it. The vendor beggars, so familiar a sight a few years ago, have all but disappeared, and you may walk from Waterloo Station to the Haymarket without so much as meeting a needy soul anxious to carry your bag. Taxicabs are in great demand. And one odd result of the scarcity of what the English are pleased to call "petrol," by which they mean gasoline, is the reappearance of that respectable, but almost obsolete animal, the family carriage-horse; of that equally obsolete vehicle, the victoria. The men on the box are invariably in black. In spite of taxes to make the hair of an American turn grey, in spite of lavish charities, the wealthy classes still seem wealthy - if the expression may be allowed. That they are not so wealthy as they were goes without saying. In the country houses of the old aristocracy the most rigid economy prevails. There are new fortunes, undoubtedly, munitions and war fortunes made before certain measures were taken to control profits; and some establishments, including a few supported by American accumulations, still exhibit the number of men servants and amount of gold plate formerly thought adequate. But in most of these great houses maids have replaced the butlers and footmen; mansions have been given over for hospitals; gardeners are fighting in the trenches, and courts and drives of country places are often overgrown with grass and weeds.

"Yes, we do dine in public quite often," said a very great lady. "It's cheaper than keeping servants."

Two of her three sons had been killed in France, but she did not mention this. The English do not advertise their sorrows. Still another explanation when husbands and sons and brothers come back across the Channel for a few days' leave after long months in the trenches, nothing is too good for them. And when these days have flown, there is always the possibility that there may never be another leave. Not long ago I read a heart-rending article about the tragedies of the goodbyes in the stations and the terminal hotels - tragedies hidden by silence and a smile. "Well, so long," says an officer "bring back a V. C.," cries his sister from the group on the platform, and he waves his hand in deprecation as the train pulls out, lights his pipe, and pretends to be reading the Sphere.

Some evening, perchance, you happen to be in the dark street outside of Charing Cross station. An occasional hooded lamp throws a precarious gleam on a long line of men carrying - so gently - stretchers on which lie the silent forms of rich and poor alike.

CHAPTER II

For the student of history who is able to place himself within the stream of evolution the really important events of today are not taking place on the battle lines, but behind them. The key-note of the new era has been struck in Russia. And as I write these words, after the Italian retreat, a second revolution seems possible. For three years one has thought inevitably of 1789, and of the ensuing world conflict out of which issued the beginnings of democracy. History does not repeat itself, yet evolution is fairly consistent. While our attention has been focused on the military drama enacted before our eyes and recorded in the newspapers, another drama, unpremeditated but of vastly greater significance, is unfolding itself behind the stage. Never in the history of the world were generals and admirals, statesmen and politicians so sensitive to or concerned about public opinion as they are today. From a military point of view the situation of the Allies at the present writing is far from reassuring. Germany and her associates have the advantage of interior lines, of a single dominating and purposeful leadership, while our five big nations, democracies or semi-democracies, are stretched in a huge ring with precarious connections on land, with the submarine alert on the sea. Much of their territory is occupied. They did not seek the war; they still lack co-ordination and leadership in waging it. In some of these countries, at least, politicians and statesmen are so absorbed by administrative duties, by national rather than international problems, by the effort to sustain themselves, that they have little time for allied strategy. Governments rise and fall, familiar names and reputations are juggled about like numbered balls in a shaker, come to the top to be submerged again in a new 'emeute'. There are conferences and conferences without end. Meanwhile a social ferment is at work, in Russia conspicuously, in Italy a little less so, in Germany and Austria undoubtedly, in France and England, and even in our own country - once of the most radical in the world, now become the most conservative.

What form will the social revolution take? Will it be unbridled, unguided; will it run through a long period of anarchy before the fermentation begun shall have been completed, or shall it be handled, in all the nations concerned, by leaders who understand and sympathize with the evolutionary trend, who are capable of controlling it, of taking the necessary international steps of co-operation in order that it may become secure and mutually beneficial to all? This is an age of co-operation, and in this at least, if not in other matters, the United States of America is in an ideal position to assume the leadership.

To a certain extent, one is not prepared to say how far, the military and social crises are interdependent. And undoubtedly the military problem rests on the suppression of the submarine. If Germany continues to destroy shipping on the seas, if we are not able to supply our new armies and the Allied nations with food and other things, the increasing social ferment will paralyze the military operations of the Entente.

The result of a German victory under such circumstances is impossible to predict; but the chances are certainly not worth running. In a, sense, therefore, in a great sense, the situation is "up" to us in more ways than one, not only to supply wise democratic leadership but to contribute material aid and brains in suppressing the submarine, and to build ships enough to keep Britain, France, and Italy from starving. We are looked upon by all the Allies, and I believe justly, as being a disinterested nation, free from the age-long jealousies of Europe. And we can do much in bringing together and making more purposeful the various elements represented by the nations to whose aid we have come.

I had not intended in these early papers to comment, but to confine myself to such of my experiences abroad as might prove interesting and somewhat illuminating. So much I cannot refrain from saying.

It is a pleasure to praise where praise is due, and too much cannot be said of the personnel of our naval service - something of which I can speak from intimate personal experience. In these days, in that part of London near the Admiralty, you may chance to run across a tall, erect, and broad-shouldered man in blue uniform with three stars on his collar, striding rapidly along the sidewalk, and sometimes, in his haste, cutting across a street. People smile at him - costermongers, clerks, and shoppers - and whisper among themselves, "There goes the American admiral!" and he invariably smiles back at them, especially at the children. He is an admiral, every inch a seaman, commanding a devoted loyalty from his staff and from the young men who are scouring the seas with our destroyers. In France as well as in England the name Sims is a household word, and if he chose he might be feted every day of the week. He does not choose. He spends long hours instead in the quarters devoted to his administration in Grosvenor Gardens, or in travelling in France and Ireland supervising the growing forces under his command.

It may not be out of place to relate a characteristic story of Admiral Sims, whose career in our service, whose notable contributions to naval gunnery are too well known to need repetition. Several years ago, on a memorable trip to England, he was designated by the admiral of the fleet to be present at a banquet given our sailors in the Guildhall. Of course the lord mayor called upon him for a speech, but Commander Sims insisted that a bluejacket should make the address. "What, a bluejacket!" exclaimed the lord mayor in astonishment. "Do bluejackets make speeches in your country?" "Certainly they do," said Sims. "Now there's a fine-looking man over there, a quartermaster on my ship. Let's call on him and see what he has to say." The quartermaster, duly summoned, rose with aplomb and delivered himself of a speech that made the hall ring, that formed the subject of a puzzled and amazed comment by the newspapers of the British Capital. Nor was it ever divulged that Commander Sims had foreseen the occasion and had picked out the impressive quartermaster to make a reputation for oratory for the enlisted force.

As a matter of fact, it is no exaggeration to add that there were and are other non-commissioned officers and enlisted men in the service who could have acquitted themselves equally well. One has only to attend some of their theatrical performances to be assured of it.

But to the European mind our bluejacket is still something of an anomaly. He is a credit to our public schools, a fruit of our system of universal education. And he belongs to a service in which are reconciled, paradoxically, democracy and discipline. One moment you may hear a bluejacket talking to an officer as man to man, and the next you will see him salute and obey an order implicitly.

On a wet and smoky night I went from the London streets into the brightness and warmth of that refuge for American soldiers and sailors, the "Eagle Hut," as the Y. M. C. A. is called. The place was full, as usual, but my glance was at once attracted by three strapping, intelligent-looking men in sailor blouses playing pool in a corner. "I simply can't get used to the fact that people like that are ordinary sailors," said the lady in charge to me as we leaned against the soda-fountain. "They're a continual pride and delight to us Americans here - always so willing to help when there's anything to be done, and so interesting to talk to." When I suggested that her ideas of the navy must have been derived from Pinafore she laughed. "I can't imagine using a cat-o'-nine-tails on them!" she exclaimed - and neither could I. I heard many similar comments. They are indubitably American, these sailors, youngsters with the stamp of our environment on their features, keen and self-reliant. I am not speaking now only of those who have enlisted since the war, but of those others, largely from the small towns and villages of our Middle West, who in the past dozen years or so have been recruited by an interesting and scientific system which is the result of the genius of our naval recruiting officers. In the files at Washington may be seen, carefully tabulated, the several reasons for their enlisting. Some have "friends in the service"; others wish to "perfect themselves in a trade," to "complete their education" or "see the world" - our adventurous spirit. And they are seeing it. They are also engaged in the most exciting and adventurous sport - with the exception of aerial warfare ever devised or developed - that of hunting down in all weathers over the wide spaces of the Atlantic those modern sea monsters that prey upon the Allied shipping. For the super-dreadnought is reposing behind the nets, the battle-cruiser ignominiously laying mines; and for the present at least, until some wizard shall invent a more effective method of annihilation, victory over Germany depends primarily on the airplane and the destroyer. At three o'clock one morning I stood on the crowded deck of an Irish mail-boat watching the full moon riding over Holyhead Mountain and shimmering on the Irish Sea. A few hours later, in the early light, I saw the green hills of Killarney against a washed and clearing sky, the mud-flats beside the railway shining like purple enamel. All the forenoon, in the train, I travelled through a country bathed in translucent colours, a country of green pastures dotted over with white sheep, of banked hedges and perfect trees, of shadowy blue hills in the high distance. It reminded one of nothing so much as a stained-glass-window depicting some delectable land of plenty and peace. And it was Ireland! When at length I arrived at the station of the port for which I was bound, and which the censor does not permit me to name, I caught sight of the figure of our Admiral on the platform; and the fact that I was in Ireland and not in Emmanuel's Land was brought home to me by the jolting drive we took on an "outside car," the admiral perched precariously over one wheel and I over the other. Winding up the hill by narrow roads, we reached the gates of the Admiralty House.

The house sits, as it were, in the emperor's seat of the amphitheatre of the town, overlooking the panorama of a perfect harbour. A ring of emerald hills is broken by a little gap to seaward, and in the centre is a miniature emerald isle. The ships lying at anchor seemed like children's boats in a pond. To the right, where a river empties in, were scattered groups of queer, rakish craft, each with four slanting pipes and a tiny flag floating from her halyards; a flag - as the binoculars revealed - of crimson bars and stars on a field of blue. These were our American destroyers. And in the midst of them, swinging to the tide, were the big "mother ships" we have sent over to nurse them when, after many days and nights of hazardous work at sea, they have brought their flock of transports and merchantmen safely to port. This "mothering" by repair-ships which are merely huge machine-shops afloat - this trick of keeping destroyers tuned up and constantly ready for service has inspired much favourable comment from our allies in the British service. It is an instance of our national adaptability, learned from an experience on long coasts where navy-yards are not too handy. Few landsmen understand how delicate an instrument the destroyer is.

A service so hazardous, demanding as it does such qualities as the ability to make instantaneous decisions and powers of mental and physical endurance, a service so irresistibly attractive to the young and adventurous, produces a type of officer quite unmistak-able. The day I arrived in London from France, seeking a characteristically English meal, I went to Simpson's in the Strand, where I found myself seated by the side of two very junior officers of the British navy. It appeared that they were celebrating what was left of a precious leave. At a neighbouring table they spied two of our officers, almost equally youthful. "Let's have 'em over," suggested one of the Britishers; and they were "had" over; he raised his glass. "Here's how - as you say in America!" he exclaimed. "You destroyer chaps are certainly top hole." And then he added, with a blush, "I say, I hope you don't think I'm cheeking you!"

I saw them afloat, I saw them coming ashore in that Irish port, these young destroyer captains, after five wakeful nights at sea, weather-bitten, clear-eyed, trained down to the last ounce. One, with whom I had played golf on the New England hills, carried his clubs in his hand and invited me to have a game with him. Another, who apologized for not being dressed at noon on Sunday - he had made the harbour at three that morning! - was taking his racquet out of its case, preparing to spend the afternoon on the hospitable courts of Admiralty House with a fellow captain and two British officers. He was ashamed of his late rising, but when it was suggested that some sleep was necessary he explained that, on the trip just ended, it wasn't only the submarines that kept him awake. "When these craft get jumping about in a seaway you can't sleep even if you want to." He who has had experience with them knows the truth of this remark. Incidentally, though he did not mention it, this young captain was one of three who had been recommended by the British admiral to his government for the Distinguished Service Order. The captain's report, which I read, is terse, and needs to be visualized. There is simply a statement of the latitude and longitude, the time of day, the fact that the wave of a periscope was sighted at 1,500 yards by the quartermaster first class on duty; general quarters rung, the executive officer signals full speed ahead, the commanding officer takes charge and manoeuvres for position - and then something happens which the censor may be fussy about mentioning. At any rate, oil and other things rise to the surface of the sea, and the Germans are minus another submarine. The chief machinist's mate, however, comes in for special mention. It seems that he ignored the ladder and literally fell down the hatch, dislocating his shoulder but getting the throttle wide open within five seconds!

In this town, facing the sea, is a street lined with quaint houses painted in yellows and browns and greens, and under each house the kind of a shop that brings back to the middleaged delectable memories of extreme youth and nickels to spend. Up and down that street on a bright Saturday afternoon may be seen our Middle-Western jackies chumming with the British sailors and Tommies, or flirting with the Irish girls, or gazing through the little panes of the show-windows, whose enterprising proprietors have imported from the States a popular brand of chewing-gum to make us feel more at home. In one of these shops, where I went to choose a picture post-card, I caught sight of an artistic display of a delicacy I had thought long obsolete - the everlasting gum-drop. But when I produced a shilling the shopkeeper shook his head. "Sure, every day the sailors are wanting to buy them of me, but it's for ornament I'm keeping them," he said. "There's no more to be had till the war will be over. Eight years they're here now, and you wouldn't get a tooth in them, sir! "So I wandered out again, joined the admiral, and inspected the Bluejackets' Club by the water's edge. Nothing one sees, perhaps, is so eloquent of the change that has taken place in the life and fabric of our navy. If you are an enlisted man, here in this commodious group of buildings you can get a good shore meal and entertain your friends among the Allies, you may sleep in a real bed, instead of a hammock, you may play pool, or see a moving-picture show, or witness a vaudeville worthy of professionals, like that recently given in honour of the visit of the admiral of our Atlantic fleet. A band of thirty pieces furnished the music, and in the opinion of the jackies one feature alone was lacking to make the entertainment a complete success - the new drop-curtain had failed to arrive from London. I happened to be present when this curtain was first unrolled, and beheld spread out before me a most realistic presentation of "little old New York," seen from the North River, towering against blue American skies. And though I have never been overfond of New York, that curtain in that place gave me a sensation!

Such is the life of our officers and sailors in these strange times that have descended upon us. Five to eight days of vigilance, of hardship and danger - in short, of war - and then three days of relaxation and enjoyment in clubs, on golf-courses and tennis-courts, barring the time it takes to clean ship and paint. There need be no fear that the war will be neglected. It is eminently safe to declare that our service will be true to its traditions.

III

"Dogged does it" ought to be added to "Dieu et mon droit" and other devices of England. On a day when I was lunching with Mr. Lloyd George in the dining-room at 10 Downing Street that looks out over the Horse Guards' Parade, the present premier, with a characteristic gesture, flung out his hand toward the portrait of a young man in the panel over the mantel. It was of the younger Pitt, who had taken his meals and drunk his port in this very room in that other great war a hundred years ago. The news of Austerlitz, brought to him during his illness, is said to have killed him. But England, undismayed, fought on for a decade, and won. Mr. Lloyd George, in spite of burdens even heavier than Pitt's, happily retains his health; and his is the indomitable spirit characteristic of the new Britain as well as of the old. For it is a new Britain one sees. Mr. Lloyd George is prime minister of a transformed Britain, a Britain modernized and democratized. Like the Englishman who, when he first witnessed a performance of "Uncle Tom's Cabin," cried out, "How very unlike the home life of our dear Queen!" the American who lunches in Downing Street is inclined to exclaim: "How different from Lord North and Palmerston!" We have, I fear, been too long accustomed to interpret Britain in terms of these two ministers and of what they represented to us of the rule of a George the Third or of an inimical aristocracy. Three out of the five men who form the war cabinet of an empire are of what would once have been termed an "humble origin." One was, if I am not mistaken, born in Nova Scotia. General Smuts, unofficially associated with this council, not many years ago was in arms against Britain in South Africa, and the prime minister himself is the son of a Welsh tailor. A situation that should mollify the most exacting and implacable of our anti-British democrats!

I listened to many speeches and explanations of the prejudice that existed in the mind of the dyed-in-the-wool American against England, and the reason most frequently given was the "school-book" reason; our histories kept the feeling alive. Now; there is no doubt that the histories out of which we were taught made what psychologists would call "action patterns," or "complexes," in our brains, just as the school-books have made similar complexes in the brains of German children and prepared them for this war. But, after all, there was a certain animus behind the histories. Boiled down, the sentiment was one against the rule of a hereditary aristocracy, and our forefathers had it long before the separation took place. The Middle-Western farmer has no prejudice against France, because France is a republic. The French are lovable, and worthy of all the sympathy and affection we can give them. But Britain is still nominally a monarchy; and our patriot thinks of its people very much as the cowboy used to regard citizens of New York. They all lived on Fifth Avenue. For the cowboy, the residents of the dreary side streets simply did not exist. We have been wont to think of all the British as aristocrats, while they have returned the compliment by visualizing all Americans as plutocrats - despite the fact that one-tenth of our population is said to own nine-tenths of all our wealth!

But the war will change that, is already changing it.

'Tout comprendre c'est tout pardonner'. We have been soaked in the same common law, literature, and traditions of liberty - or of chaos, as one likes. Whether we all be of British origin or not, it is the mind that makes the true patriot; and there is no American so dead as not to feel a thrill when he first sets foot on British soil. Our school-teachers felt it when they began to travel some twenty years ago, and the thousands of our soldiers who pass through on their way to France are feeling it today, and writing home about it. Our soldiers and sailors are being cared for and entertained in England just as they would be cared for and entertained at home. So are their offcers. Not long ago one of the finest town houses in London was donated by the owner for an American officers' club, the funds were raised by contributions from British officers, and the club was inaugurated by the King and Queen - and Admiral Sims. Hospitality and good-will have gone much further than this. Any one who knows London will understand the sacredness of those private squares, surrounded by proprietary residences, where every tree and every blade of grass has been jealously guarded from intrusion for a century or more. And of all these squares that of St. James's is perhaps the most exclusive, and yet it is precisely in St. James's there is to be built the first of those hotels designed primarily for the benefit of American officers, where they can get a good room for five shillings a night and breakfast at a reasonable price. One has only to sample the war-time prices of certain hostelries to appreciate the value of this.

On the first of four unforgettable days during which I was a guest behind the British lines in France the officer who was my guide stopped the motor in the street of an old village, beside a courtyard surrounded by ancient barns.

"There are some of your Americans," he remarked.

I had recognized them, not by their uniforms but by their type. Despite their costumes, which were negligible, they were eloquent of college campuses in every one of our eight and forty States, lean, thin-hipped, alert. The persistent rains had ceased, a dazzling sunlight made that beautiful countryside as bright as a coloured picture post-card, but a riotous cold gale was blowing; yet all wore cotton trousers that left their knees as bare as Highlanders' kilts. Above these some had an sweaters, others brown khaki tunics, from which I gathered that they belonged to the officers' training corps. They were drawn up on two lines facing each other with fixed bayonets, a grim look on their faces that would certainly have put any Hun to flight. Between the files stood an unmistakable gipling sergeant with a crimson face and a bristling little chestnut moustache, talking like a machine gun.

"Now, then, not too lidylike! - there's a Bosch in front of you! Run 'im through! Now, then!"

The lines surged forward, out went the bayonets, first the long thrust and then the short, and then a man's gun was seized and by a swift backward twist of the arm he was made helpless.

"Do you feel it?" asked the officer, as he turned to me. I did.
"Up and down your spine," he added, and I nodded. "Those chaps will do," he said. He had been through that terrible battle of the Somme, and he knew. So had the sergeant.

Presently came a resting-spell. One of the squad

approached me, whom I recognized as a young man I had met in the Harvard Union.

"If you write about this," he said, "just tell our people that we're going to take that sergeant home with us when the war's over. He's too good to lose."

IV

It is trite to observe that democracies are organized - if, indeed, they are organized at all - not for war but for peace. And nowhere is this fact more apparent than in Britain. Even while the war is in progress has that internal democratic process of evolution been going on, presaging profound changes in the social fabric. And these changes must be dealt with by statesmen, must be guided with one hand while the war is being prosecuted with the other. The task is colossal. In no previous war have the British given more striking proof of their inherent quality of doggedness. Greatness, as Confucius said, does not consist in never falling, but in rising every time you fall. The British speak with appalling frankness of their blunders. They are fighting, indeed, for the privilege of making blunders - since out of blunders arise new truths and discoveries not contemplated in German philosophy.

America must now contribute what Britain and France, with all their energies and resources and determination, have hitherto been unable to contribute. It must not be men, money, and material alone, but some quality that America has had in herself during her century and a half of independent self-realization. Mr. Chesterton, in writing about the American Revolution, observes that the real case for the colonists is that they felt that they could be something which England would not help them to be. It is, in fact, the only case for separation. What may be called the English tradition of democracy, which we inherit, grows through conflicts and differences, through experiments and failures and successes, toward an intellectualized unity, -

experiments by states, experiments by individuals, a widely spread development, and new contributions to the whole.

Democracy has arrived at the stage when it is ceasing to be national and selfish.

It must be said of England, in her treatment of her colonies subsequent to our Revolution, that she took this greatest of all her national blunders to heart. As a result, Canada and Australia and New Zealand have sent their sons across the seas to fight for an empire that refrains from coercion; while, thanks to the policy of the British Liberals - which was the expression of the sentiment of the British nation - we have the spectacle today of a Botha and a Smuts fighting under the Union Jack.

And how about Ireland? England has blundered there, and she admits it freely. They exist in England who cry out for the coercion of Ireland, and who at times have almost had their way. But to do this, of course, would be a surrender to the German contentions, an acknowledgment of the wisdom of the German methods against which she is protesting with all her might. Democracy, apparently, must blunder on until that question too, is solved.

V

Many of those picturesque features of the older England, that stir us by their beauty and by the sense of stability and permanence they convey, will no doubt disappear or be transformed. I am thinking of the great estates, some of which date from Norman times; I am thinking of the aristocracy, which we Americans repudiated in order to set up a plutocracy instead. Let us hope that what is fine in it will be preserved, for there is much. By the theory of the British constitution - that unwritten but very real document - in return for honours, emoluments, and titles, the burden of government has hitherto been thrown on a class. Nor can it be said that they have been untrue to their responsibility. That class developed a tradition and held fast to it; and they had a foreign policy that guided England through centuries of greatness. Democracy too must have a foreign policy, a tradition of service; a trained if not hereditary group to guide it through troubled waters. Even in an intelligent community there must be leadership. And, if the world will no longer tolerate the old theories, a tribute may at least be paid to those who from conviction upheld them; who ruled, perhaps in affluence, yet were also willing to toil and, if need be, to die for the privilege.

One Saturday afternoon, after watching for a while the boys playing fives and football and romping over the green lawns at Eton, on my way to the head master's rooms I paused in one of the ancient quads. My eye had been caught by a long column of names posted there, printed in heavy black letters. 'Etona non, immemora'! Every week many new names are added to those columns. On the walls of the chapel and in other quads and passages may be found tablets and inscriptions in memory of those who have died for England and the empire in by-gone wars. I am told that the proportion of Etonians of killed to wounded is greater than that of any other public school - which is saying a great deal. They go back across the channel and back again until their names appear on the last and highest honour list of the school and nation.

In one of the hospitals I visited lay a wounded giant who had once been a truckman in a little town in Kent. Incidentally, in common with his neighbours, he had taken no interest in the war, which had seemed as remote to him as though he had lived in North Dakota. One day a Zeppelin dropped a bomb on that village, whereupon the able-bodied males enlisted to a man, and he with them. A subaltern in his company was an Eton boy. "We just couldn't think of 'im as an orficer, sir; in the camps 'e used to play with us like a child. And then we went to France. And one night when we was wet to the skin and the Boschs was droppin' shell all around us we got the word. It was him leaped over the top first of all, shouting back at us to come on. He tumbled right back and died in my arms, 'e did, as I was climbin' up after 'im. I shan't ever forget 'im."

As you travel about in these days you become conscious, among the people you meet, of a certain bewilderment. A static world and a static order are dissolving; and in England that order was so static as to make the present spectacle the more surprising. Signs of the disintegration of the old social strata were not lacking, indeed, in the earlier years of the twentieth century, when labour members and north-country radicals began to invade parliament; but the cataclysm

of this war has accelerated the process. In the muddy
trenches of Flanders and France a new comradeship
has sprung up between officers and Tommies, while
time-honoured precedent has been broken by the
necessity of giving thousands of commissions to men
of merit who do not belong to the "officer caste." At
the Haymarket Theatre I saw a fashionable audience
wildly applaud a play in which the local tailor becomes
a major-general and returns home to marry the
daughter of the lord of a mayor whose clothes he used
to cut before the war.

"The age of great adventure," were the words used by
Mr. H. G. Wells to describe this epoch as we discussed
it. And a large proportion of the descendants of those
who have governed England for centuries are
apparently imbued with the spirit of this adventure,
even though it may spell the end of their exclusive
rule. As significant of the social mingling of elements
which in the past never exchanged ideas or points of
view I shall describe a week-end party at a large
country house of Liberal complexion; on the Thames. I
have reason to believe it fairly typical. The owner of
this estate holds an important position in the Foreign
Office, and the hostess has, by her wit and intelligent
grasp of affairs, made an enviable place for herself. On
her right, at luncheon on Sunday, was a labour leader,
the head of one of the most powerful unions in Britain,
and next him sat a member of one of the oldest of
England's titled families. The two were on terms of
Christian names. The group included two or three
women, a sculptor and an educator, another Foreign
Office official who has made a reputation since the
beginning of the war, and finally an employer of
labour, the chairman of the biggest shipbuilding
company in England.

That a company presenting such a variety of interests should have been brought together in the frescoed dining-room of that particular house is noteworthy.

The thing could happen nowhere save in the England of today. At first the talk was general, ranging over a number of subjects from that of the personality of certain politicians to the conduct of the war and the disturbing problem raised by the "conscientious objector"; little by little, however, the rest of us became silent, to listen to a debate which had begun between the labour leader and the ship-builder on the "labour question." It is not my purpose here to record what they said. Needless to add that they did not wholly agree, but they were much nearer to agreement than one would have thought possible. What was interesting was the open-mindedness with which, on both sides, the argument was conducted, and the fact that it could seriously take place then and there. For the subject of it had long been the supreme problem in the lives of both these men, their feelings concerning it must at times have been tinged with bitterness, yet they spoke with courtesy and restraint, and though each maintained his contentions he was quick to acknowledge a point made by the other. As one listened one was led to hope that a happier day is perhaps at hand when such things as "complexes" and convictions will disappear.

The types of these two were in striking contrast. The labour leader was stocky, chestnut-coloured, vital, possessing the bulldog quality of the British self-made man combined with a natural wit, sharpened in the arena, that often startled the company into an appreciative laughter. The ship-builder, on the other hand, was one of those spare and hard Englishmen whom no amount of business cares will induce to neglect the exercise of his body, the obligation at all times to keep "fit"; square-rigged, as it were, with a lean face and a wide moustache accentuating a square chin. Occasionally a gleam of humour, a ray of idealism, lighted his practical grey eyes. Each of these two had managed rather marvellously to triumph over early training by self-education: the labour leader, who had had his first lessons in life from injustices and hard knocks; and the ship-builder, who had overcome the handicap of the public-school tradition and of Manchester economics.

"Yes, titles and fortunes must go," remarked our hostess with a smile as she rose from the table and led the way out on the sunny, stone-flagged terrace. Below us was a wide parterre whose flower-beds, laid out by a celebrated landscape-gardener in the days of the Stuarts, were filled with vegetables. The day was like our New England Indian summerthough the trees were still heavy with leaves - and a gossamer-blue veil of haze stained the hills between which the shining river ran. If the social revolution, or evolution, takes place, one wonders what will become of this long-cherished beauty.

I venture to dwell upon one more experience of that week-end party. The Friday evening of my arrival I was met at the station, not by a limousine with a chauffeur and footman, but by a young woman with a taxicab - one of the many reminders that a war is going on. London had been reeking in a green-yellow fog, but here the mist was white, and through it I caught glimpses of the silhouettes of stately trees in a park, and presently saw the great house with its clock-tower looming up before me. A fire was crackling in the hall, and before it my hostess was conversing amusedly with a well-known sculptor - a sculptor typical of these renaissance times, large, full-blooded, with vigorous opinions on all sorts of matters.

"A lecturer is coming down from London to talk to the wounded in the amusement-hall of the hospital," our hostess informed us. "And you both must come and speak too."

The three of us got into the only motor of which the establishment now boasts, a little runabout using a minimum of "petrol," and she guided us rapidly by devious roads through the fog until a blur of light proclaimed the presence of a building, one of some score or more built on the golf- course by the British Government. I have not space hereto describe that hospital, which is one of the best in England; but it must be observed that its excellence and the happiness of its inmates are almost wholly due to the efforts of the lady who now conducted us across the stage of the amusement-hall, where all the convalescents who could walk or who could be rolled thither in chairs were gathered. The lecturer had not arrived. But the lady of the manor seated herself at the speaker's table, singling out Scotch wits in the audience - for whom she was more than a match - while the sculptor and I looked on and grinned and resisted her blandishments to make speeches. When at last the lecturer came he sat down informally on the table with one foot hanging in the air and grinned, too, at her bantering but complimentary introduction. It was then I discovered for the first time that he was one of the best educational experts of that interesting branch of the British Government, the Department of Reconstruction, whose business it is to teach the convalescents the elements of social and political science. This was not to be a lecture, he told them, but a debate in which every man must take a part. And his first startling question was this:

"Why should Mr. Lloyd George, instead of getting five thousand pounds a year for his services as prime minister, receive any more than a common labourer?"

The question was a poser. The speaker folded his hands and beamed down at them; he seemed fairly to radiate benignity.

"Now we mustn't be afraid of him, just because he seems to be intelligent," declared our hostess. This sally was greeted with spasmodic laughter. Her eyes flitted from bench to bench, yet met nothing save averted glances. "Jock! Where are you, Jock? Why don't you speak up? - you've never been downed before."

More laughter, and craning of necks for the Jocks. This appeared to be her generic name for the vita. But the Jocks remained obdurately modest. The prolonged silence did not seem in the least painful to the lecturer, who thrust his hand in his pocket and continued to beam. He had learned how to wait. And at last his patience was rewarded. A middleaged soldier with a very serious manner arose hesitatingly, with encouraging noises from his comrades.

"It's not Mr. Lloyd George I'm worrying about, sir," he said, "all I wants is enough for the missus and me. I had trouble to get that before the war."

Cries of "Hear! Hear!"

"Why did you have trouble?" inquired the lecturer mildly.

"The wages was too low."

"And why were the wages too low?"

"You've got me there. I hadn't thought."

"But isn't it your business as a voter to think?" asked the lecturer. "That's why the government is sending me here, to start you to thinking, to remind you that it is you soldiers who will have to take charge of this country and run it after the war is over. And you won't be able to do that unless you think, and think straight."

"We've never been taught to think," was the illuminating reply.

"And if we do think we've never been educated to express ourselves, same as you!" shouted another man, in whom excitement had overcome timidity.

"I'm here to help you educate yourselves," said the lecturer. "But first let's hear any ideas you may have on the question I asked you."

There turned out to be plenty of ideas, after all. An opinion was ventured that Mr. Lloyd George served the nation, not for money but from public spirit; a conservative insisted that ability should be rewarded and rewarded well; whereupon ensued one of the most enlightening discussions, not only as a revelation of intelligence, but of complexes and obsessions pervading many of the minds in whose power lies the ultimate control of democracies. One, for instance, declared that - "if every man went to church proper of a Sunday and minded his own business the country would get along well enough." He was evidently of the opinion that there was too much thinking and not enough of what he would have termed "religion." Gradually that audience split up into liberals and conservatives; and the liberals noticeably were the younger men who had had the advantages of better board schools, who had formed fewer complexes and had had less time in which to get them set. Of these, a Canadian made a plea for the American system of universal education, whereupon a combative "stand-patter" declared that every man wasn't fit to be educated, that the American plan made only for discontent. "Look at them," he exclaimed, "They're never satisfied to stay in their places." This provoked laughter, but it was too much for the sculptor - and for me. We both broke our vows and made speeches in favour of equality and mental opportunity, while the lecturer looked on and smiled. Mr. Lloyd George and his salary were forgotten. By some subtle art of the chairman the debate had been guided to the very point where he had from the first intended to guide it - to the burning question of our day - education as the true foundation of democracy! Perhaps, after all, this may be our American contribution to the world's advance.

As we walked homeward through the fog I talked to him of Professor Dewey's work and its results, while he explained to me the methods of the Reconstruction Department. "Out of every audience like that we get a group and form a class," he said. "They're always a bit backward at first, just as they were tonight, but they grow very keen. We have a great many classes already started, and we see to it that they are provided with text-books and teachers. Oh, no, it's not propaganda," he added, in answer to my query; "all we do is to try to give them facts in such a way as to make them able to draw their own conclusions and join any political party they choose - just so they join one intelligently." I must add that before Sunday was over he had organized his class and arranged for their future instruction.

CHAPTER III

I would speak first of a contrast - and yet I have come to recognize how impossible it is to convey to the dweller in America the difference in atmosphere between England and France on the one hand and our country on the other. And when I use the word "atmosphere" I mean the mental state of the peoples as well as the weather and the aspect of the skies. I have referred in another article to the anxious, feverish prosperity one beholds in London and Paris, to that apparent indifference, despite the presence on the streets of crowds of soldiers to the existence of a war of which one is ever aware. Yet, along with this, one is ever conscious of pressure. The air is heavy; there is a corresponding lack of the buoyancy of mind which is the normal American condition. Perhaps, if German troops occupied New England and New York, our own mental barometer might be lower. It is difficult to say. At any rate, after an ocean voyage of nine days one's spirits rise perceptibly as the ship nears Nantucket; and the icy-bright sunlight of New York harbour, the sight of the buildings aspiring to blue skies restore the throbbing optimism which with us is normal; and it was with an effort, when I talked to the reporters on landing, that I was able to achieve and express the pessimism and darkness out of which I had come. Pessimism is perhaps too strong a word, and takes no account of the continued unimpaired morale and determination of the greater part of the British and French peoples. They expect much from us. Yet the impression was instantaneous, when I set forth in the streets of New York, that we had not fully measured the magnitude of our task - an impression that has been amply confirmed as the weeks have passed.

The sense of relief I felt was not only the result of bright skies and a high barometer, of the palpable self-confidence of the pedestrians, of the white bread on the table and the knowledge that there was more, but also of the ease of accomplishing things. I called for a telephone number and got it cheerfully and instantly. I sent several telegrams, and did not have to wait twenty minutes before a wicket while a painstaking official multiplied and added and subtracted and paused to talk with a friend; the speed of the express in which I flew down-town seemed emblematic of America itself. I had been transported, in fact, into another world - my world; and in order to realize again that from which I had come I turned to a diary recording a London filled with the sulphur fumes of fog, through which the lamps of the taxis and buses shone as yellow blots reflected on glistening streets; or, for some reason a still greater contrast, a blue, blue November Sunday afternoon in parts, the Esplanade of the Invalides black with people - sad people - and the Invalides itself all etched in blue as seen through the wide vista from the Seine.

A few days later, with some children, I went to the Hippodrome. And it remained for the Hippodrome, of all places, to give me the thrill I had not achieved abroad, the thrill I had not experienced since the first months of the war. Mr. George Cohan accomplished it. The transport with steam up, is ready to leave the wharf, the khaki-clad regiment of erect and vigorous young Americans marches across the great stage, and the audience strains forward and begins to sing, under its breath, the words that proclaim, as nothing else perhaps proclaims, how America feels.

"Send the word, send the word over there . . .
We'll be o-ver, we're coming o-ver,
And we won't come back till it's o-ver, over there!"

Is it the prelude of a tragedy? We have always been so successful, we Americans. Are we to fail now? I am an American, and I do not believe we are to fail. But I am soberer, somehow a different American than he who sailed away in August. Shall we learn other things than those that have hitherto been contained in our philosophy?

Of one thing I am convinced. It is the first war of the world that is not a miltary war, although miltary genius is demanded, although it is the bloodiest war in history. But other qualities are required; men and women who are not professional soldiers are fighting in it and will aid in victory. The pomp and circumstance of other wars are lacking in this, the greatest of all. We had the thrills, even in America, three years ago, when Britain and France and Canada went in. We tingled when we read of the mobilizing of the huge armies, of the leave-takings of the soldiers. We bought every extra for news of those first battles on Belgian soil. And I remember my sensations when in the province of Quebec in the autumn of 1914, looking out of the car-window at the troops gathering on the platforms who were to go across the seas to fight for the empire and liberty. They were singing "Tipperary!" "Tipperary!" One seldoms hears it now, and the way has proved long - longer than we reckoned. And we are singing "Over There!"

In those first months of the war there was, we were told, in England and France a revival of "religion," and indeed many of the books then written gave evidence of having been composed in exalted, mystic moods. I remember one in particular, called "En Campagne," by a young French officer. And then, somehow, the note of mystic exaltation died away, to be succeeded by a period of realism. Read "Le Feu," which is most typical, which has sold in numberless editions. Here is a picture of that other aspect - the grimness, the monotony, and the frequent bestiality of trench life, the horror of slaughtering millions of men by highly specialized machinery. And yet, as an American, I strike inevitably the note of optimism once more. Even now the truer spiritual goal is glimpsed through the battle clouds, and has been hailed in world-reverberating phrases by our American President. Day by day the real issue is clearer, while the "religion" it implies embraces not one nation, wills not one patriotism, but humanity itself. I heard a Frenchwoman who had been deeply "religious" in the old sense exclaim: "I no longer have any faith in God; he is on the side of the Germans." When the war began there were many evidences of a survival of that faith that God fights for nations, interferes in behalf of the "righteous" cause. When General Joffre was in America he was asked by one of our countrywomen how the battle of the Marne was won. "Madame," he is reported to have said, "it was won by me, by my generals and soldiers." The tendency to regard this victory, which we hope saved France and the Western humanitarian civilization we cherish, as a special interposition of Providence, as a miracle, has given place to the realization that the battle was won by the resourcefulness, science, and coolness of the French commander-in-chief. Science preserves armies, since killing, if it has to be done, is now wholly within that realm; science heals the wounded, transports them rapidly to the hospitals, gives the shattered something still to live for; and, if we are able to abandon the sentimental view and look facts in the face - as many anointed chaplains in Europe are doing - science not only eliminates typhoid but is able to prevent those terrible diseases that devastate armies and nations. And science is no longer confined to the physical but has invaded the social kingdom, is able to weave a juster fabric into the government of peoples. On all sides we are beginning to embrace the religion of self-reliance, a faith that God is on the side of intelligence - intelligence with a broader meaning than the Germans have given it, for it includes charity.

II

It seems to me that I remember, somewhere in the realistic novel I have mentioned "Le Feu" - reading of singing soldiers, and an assumption on the part of their hearers that such songs are prompted only by a devil-may-care lightness of heart which the soldier achieves. A shallow psychology (as the author points out), especially in these days of trench warfare! The soldier sings to hide his real feelings, perhaps to give vent to them. I am reminded of all this in connection with my trip to the British front. I left London after lunch on one of those dreary, grey days to which I have referred; the rain had begun to splash angrily against the panes of the car windows before we reached the coast. At five o'clock the boat pushed off into a black channel, whipped by a gale that drove the rain across the decks and into every passage and gangway. The steamer was literally loaded with human beings, officers and men returning from a brief glimpse of home. There was nothing of the glory of war in the embarkation, and, to add to the sad and sinister effect of it, each man as he came aboard mounted the ladder and chose, from a pile on the hatch combing, a sodden life-preserver, which he flung around his shoulders as he went in search of a shelter. The saloon below, where we had our tea, was lighted indeed, but sealed so tight as to be insupportable; and the cabin above, stifling too, was dark as a pocket. One stumbled over unseen passengers on the lounges, or sitting on kits on the floor. Even the steps up which I groped my way to the deck above were filled, while on the deck there was standing-room only and not much of that. Mal de mer added to the discomforts of many. At length I found an uncertain refuge in a gangway amidships, hedged in between unseen companions; but even here the rain stung our faces and the spray of an occasional comber drenched our feet, while through the gloom of the night only a few yards of white water were to be discerned. For three hours I stood there, trying to imagine what was in the minds of these men with whose bodies I was in such intimate contact. They were going to a foreign land to fight, many of them to die, not in one of those adventurous campaigns of times gone by, but in the wet trenches or the hideous No Man's Land between. What were the images they summoned up in the darkness? Visions of long-familiar homes and long-familiar friends? And just how were they facing the future? Even as I wondered, voices rose in a song, English voices, soldier voices. It was not "Tipperary," the song that thrilled us a few years ago. I strove to catch the words:

> "I want to go home!
> I don't want to go back to the trenches no more,
> Where there are bullets and shrapnel galore,
> I want to go home!"

It was sung boisterously, in a defiant tone of mockery of the desire it expressed, and thus tremendously gained in pathos. They did want to go home - naturally. It was sung with the same spirit our men sing "We won't come back till it's over, over there!" The difference is that these Britishers have been over there, have seen the horrors face to face, have tasted the sweets of home, and in spite of heartsickness and seasickness are resolved to see it through. Such is the morale of the British army. I have not the slightest doubt that it will be the morale of our own army also, but at present the British are holding the fort. Tommy would never give up the war, but he has had a realistic taste of it, and his songs reflect his experience. Other songs reached my ears each night, above the hissing and pounding of the Channel seas, but the unseen group returned always to this. One thought of Agincourt and Crecy, of Waterloo, of the countless journeys across this same stormy strip of water the ancestors of these man had made in the past, and one wondered whether war were eternal and inevitable, after all.

And what does Tommy think about it - this war? My own limited experience thoroughly indorses Mr. Galsworthy's splendid analysis of British-soldier psychology that appeared in the December North American. The average man, with native doggedness, is fighting for the defence of England. The British Government itself, in its reconstruction department for the political education of the wounded, has given partial denial to the old maxim that it is the soldier's business not to think but to obey; and the British army is leavened with men who read and reflect in the long nights of watching in the rain, who are gaining ideas about conditions in the past and resolutions concerning those of the future. The very army itself has had a miracle happen to it: it has been democratized - and with the cheerful consent of the class to which formerly the possession of commissions was largely confined. Gradually, to these soldier-thinkers, as well as to the mass of others at home, is unfolding the vision of a new social order which is indeed worth fighting for and dying for.

III

At last, our knees cramped and our feet soaked, we saw the lights of the French port dancing across the veil of rain, like thistledowns of fire, and presently we were at rest at a stone quay. As I stood waiting on the deck to have my passport vised, I tried to reconstruct the features of this little seaport as I had seen it, many years before, on a bright summer's day when I had motored from Paris on my way to London. The gay line of hotels facing the water was hidden in the darkness. Suddenly I heard my name called, and I was rescued from the group of civilians by a British officer who introduced himself as my host. It was after nine o'clock, and he had been on the lookout for me since half past seven. The effect of his welcome at that time and place was electrical, and I was further immensely cheered by the news he gave me, as we hurried along the street, that two friends of mine were here and quite hungry, having delayed dinner for my arrival. One of them was a young member of Congress who had been making exhaustive studies of the situation in Italy, France and England, and the other one of our best-known writers, both bound for London. We sat around the table until nearly eleven, exchanging impressions and experiences. Then my officer declared that it was time to go home.

"Home" proved to be the big chateau which the British Government has leased for the kindly purpose of entertaining such American guests as they choose to invite. It is known as the "American Chateau," and in the early morning hours we reached it after a long drive through the gale. We crossed a bridge over a moat and traversed a huge stone hall to the Gothic drawing-room. Here a fire was crackling on the hearth, refreshments were laid out, and the major in command rose from his book to greet me. Hospitality, with these people, has attained to art, and, though I had come here at the invitation of his government, I had the feeling of being his personal guest in his own house. Presently he led the way up the stone stairs and showed me the room I was to occupy.

I awoke to the sound of the wind whistling through the open lattice, and looking down on the ruffled blue waters of the moat I saw a great white swan at his morning toilet, his feathers dazzling in the sun. It was one of those rare crisp and sparkling days that remind one of our American autumn. A green stretch of lawn made a vista through the woods. Following the example of the swan, I plunged into the tin tub the orderly had placed beside my bed and went down to porridge in a glow. Porridge, for the major was Scotch, and had taught his French cook to make it as the Scotch make it. Then, going out into the hall, from a table on which lay a contour map of the battle region, the major picked up a hideous mask that seemed to have been made for some barbaric revelries.

"We may not strike any gas," he said, "but it's as well to be on the safe side," whereupon he made me practise inserting the tube in my mouth, pinching the nostrils instantly with the wire-covered nippers. He also presented me with a steel helmet. Thus equipped for any untoward occurrence, putting on sweaters and heavy overcoats, and wrapping ourselves in the fur rugs of the waiting automobile, we started off, with the gale on our quarter, for the front.

Picardy, on whose soil has been shed so much English blood, never was more beautiful than on that October day. The trees were still in full leaf, the fields green, though the crops had been gathered, and the crystal air gave vivid value to every colour in the landscape. From time to time we wound through the cobble-stoned streets of historic villages, each having its stone church end the bodki-shaped steeple of blue slate so characteristic of that country. And, as though we were still in the pastoral times of peace, in the square of one of these villages a horse-fair was in progress, blue-smocked peasants were trotting chunky ponies over the stones. It was like a picture from one of De Maupassant's tales. In other villages the shawled women sat knitting behind piles of beets and cabbages and apples, their farm-carts atilt in the sun. Again and again I tried to grasp the fact that the greatest of world wars was being fought only a few miles away - and failed.

We had met, indeed, an occasional officer or orderly, huddled in a greatcoat and head against the wind, exercising those wonderful animals that are the pride of the British cavalry and which General Sir Douglas Haig, himself a cavalryman, some day hopes to bring into service. We had overtaken an artillery train rumbling along toward the east, the men laughing and joking as they rode, as though they were going to manoeuvres. Farther on, as the soldiers along the highroads and in the towns grew more and more numerous, they seemed so harmoniously part of the peaceful scene that war was as difficult to visualize as ever. Many sat about smoking their pipes and playing with the village children, others were in squads going to drill or exercise - something the Briton never neglects. The amazing thing to a visitor who has seen the trenches awash on a typical wet day, who knows that even billeting in cold farms and barns behind the lines can scarcely be compared to the comforts of home, is how these men keep well under the conditions. To say that they are well is to understate the fact: the ruddy faces and clear eyes and hard muscles - even of those who once were pale London clerks - proclaim a triumph for the system of hygiene of their army.

Suddenly we came upon a house with a great round hole in its wall, and then upon several in ruins beside the village street. Meanwhile, at work under the wind-swept trees of the highway, were strange, dark men from the uttermost parts of the earth, physiognomies as old as the tombs of Pharaoh. It was, indeed, not so much the graven red profiles of priests and soldiers that came tome at sight of these Egyptians, but the singing fellaheen of the water-buckets of the Nile. And here, too, shovelling the crushed rock, were East Indians oddly clad in European garb, careless of the cold. That sense of the vastness of the British Empire, which at times is so profound, was mingled now with a knowledge that it was fighting for its life, marshalling all its resources for Armageddon.

Saint Eloi is named after the good bishop who ventured to advise King Dagobert about his costume. And the church stands - what is left of it - all alone on the greenest of terraces jutting out toward the east; and the tower, ruggedly picturesque against the sky, resembles that of some crumbled abbey. As a matter of fact, it has been a target for German gunners. Dodging an army-truck and rounding one of those military traffic policemen one meets at every important corner we climbed the hill and left the motor among the great trees, which are still fortunately preserved. And we stood for a few minutes, gazing over miles and miles of devastation. Then, taking the motor once more, we passed through wrecked and empty villages until we came to the foot of Vimy Ridge. Notre Dame de Lorette rose against the sky-line to the north.

Vimy and Notre Dame de Lorette - sweet but terrible names! Only a summer had passed since Vimy was the scene of one of the bloodiest battles of the war. From a distance the prevailing colour of the steep slope is ochre; it gives the effect of having been scraped bare in preparation for some gigantic enterprise. A nearer view reveals a flush of green; nature is already striving to heal. From top to bottom it is pockmarked by shells and scarred by trenches - trenches every few feet, and between them tangled masses of barbed wire still clinging to the "knife rests" and corkscrew stanchions to which it had been strung. The huge shell-holes, revealing the chalk subsoil, were half-filled with water. And even though the field had been cleaned by those East Indians I had seen on the road, and the thousands who had died here buried, bits of uniform, shoes, and accoutrements and shattered rifles were sticking in the clay - and once we came across a portion of a bedstead, doubtless taken by some officer from a ruined and now vanished village to his dugout. Painfully, pausing frequently to ponder over these remnants, so eloquent of the fury of the struggle, slipping backward at every step and despite our care getting tangled in the wire, we made our way up the slope. Buttercups and daisies were blooming around the edges of the craters.

As we drew near the crest the major warned me not to expose myself. "It isn't because there is much chance of our being shot," he explained," but a matter of drawing the German fire upon others." And yet I found it hard to believe - despite the evidence at my feet - that war existed here. The brightness of the day, the emptiness of the place, the silence - save for the humming of the gale - denied it. And then, when we had cautiously rounded a hummock at the top, my steel helmet was blown off - not by a shrapnel, but by the wind! I had neglected to tighten the chin-strap.

Immediately below us I could make out scars like earthquake cracks running across the meadows - the front trenches. Both armies were buried like moles in these furrows. The country was spread out before us, like a map, with occasionally the black contour of a coal mound rising against the green, or a deserted shaft-head. I was gazing at the famous battle-field of Lens. Villages, woods, whose names came back to me as the major repeated them, lay like cloud shadows on the sunny plain, and the faintest shadow of all, far to the eastward, was Lens itself. I marked it by a single white tower. And suddenly another white tower, loftier than the first, had risen up! But even as I stared its substance seemed to change, to dissolve, and the tower was no longer to be seen. Not until then did I realize that a monster shell had burst beside the trenches in front of the city. Occasionally after that there came to my ears the muffed report of some hidden gun, and a ball like a powder-puff lay lightly on the plain, and vanished. But even the presence of these, oddly enough, did not rob the landscape of its air of Sunday peace.

We ate our sandwiches and drank our bottle of white wine in a sheltered cut of the road that runs up that other ridge which the French gained at such an appalling price, Notre Dame de Lorette, while the major described to me some features of the Lens battle, in which he had taken part. I discovered incidentally that he had been severely wounded at the Somme. Though he had been a soldier all his life, and a good soldier, his true passion was painting, and he drew my attention to the rare greens and silver-greys of the stones above us, steeped in sunlight - all that remained of the little church of Notre Dame - more beautiful, more significant, perhaps, as a ruin. It reminded the major of the Turners he had admired in his youth. After lunch we lingered in the cemetery, where the graves and vaults had been harrowed by shells; the trenches ran right through them. And here, in this desecrated resting-place of the village dead, where the shattered gravestones were mingled with barbed wire, death-dealing fragments of iron, and rusting stick-bombs that had failed to explode, was a wooden cross, on which was rudely written the name of Hans Siebert. Mouldering at the foot of the cross was a grey woollen German tunic from which the buttons had been cut.

We kept the road to the top, for Notre Dame de Lorette is as steep as Vimy. There we looked upon the panorama of the Lens battle-field once more, and started down the eastern slope, an apparently smooth expanse covered now with prairie grasses, in reality a labyrinth of deep ditches, dugouts, and pits; gruesome remnants of the battle lay half-concealed under the grass. We walked slowly, making desperate leaps over the trenches, sometimes perforce going through them, treading gingerly on the "duck board" at the bottom. We stumbled over stick-bombs and unexploded shells. No plough can be put here - the only solution for the land for years to come is forest. Just before we gained the road at the bottom, where the car was awaiting us, we were startled by the sudden flight of a covey of partridges.

The skies were grey when we reached the banal outskirts of a town where the bourgeoise houses were modern, commonplace, save those which had been ennobled by ruin. It was Arras, one of those few magic names, eloquent with suggestions of mediaeval romance and art, intrigue and chivalry; while upon their significance, since the war began, has been superimposed still another, no less eloquent but charged with pathos. We halted for a moment in the open space before the railroad station, a comparatively new structure of steel and glass, designed on geometrical curves, with an uninspiring, cheaply ornamented front. It had been, undoubtedly, the pride of the little city. Yet finding it here had at first something of the effect of the discovery of an office-building - let us say - on the site of the Reims Cathedral. Presently, however, its emptiness, its silence began to have their effects - these and the rents one began to perceive in the roof. For it was still the object of the intermittent yet persistent fire of the German artillery. One began to realize that by these wounds it had achieved a dignity that transcended the mediocre imagination of its provincial designer. A fine rain had set in before we found the square, and here indeed one felt a certain desolate satisfaction; despite the wreckage there the spirit of the ancient town still poignantly haunted it. Although the Hotel de Ville, which had expressed adequately the longings and aspirations, the civic pride of those bygone burghers, was razed to the ground, on three sides were still standing the varied yet harmonious facades of Flemish houses made familiar by photographs. Of some of these the plaster between the carved beams had been shot away, the roofs blown off, and the tiny hewn rafters were bared to the sky. The place was empty in the gathering gloom of the twilight. The gaiety and warmth of the hut erected in the Public Gardens which houses the British Officers' Club were a relief.

The experiences of the next day will remain for ever in my memory etched, as it were, in sepia. My guide was a younger officer who had seen heroic service, and I wondered constantly how his delicate frame had survived in the trenches the constant hardship of such weather as now, warmly wrapped and with the car-curtains drawn, we faced. The inevitable, relentless rain of that region had set in again, the rain in which our own soldiers will have to fight, and the skies were of a darkness seldom known in America. The countryside was no longer smiling. After some two hours of progress we came, in that devastated district near the front, to an expanse where many monsters were clumsily cavorting like dinosaurs in primeval slime. At some distance from the road others stood apparently tethered in line, awaiting their turn for exercise. These were the far-famed tanks. Their commander, or chief mahout - as I was inclined to call him - was a cheerful young giant of colonial origin, who has often driven them serenely across No Man's Land and into the German trenches. He had been expecting us, and led me along a duck board over the morass, to where one of these leviathans was awaiting us. You crawl through a greasy hole in the bottom, and the inside is as full of machinery as the turret of the Pennsylvania, and you grope your way to the seat in front beside that of the captain and conductor, looking out through a slot in the armour over a waste of water and mud. From here you are supposed to operate a machine gun. Behind you two mechanics have started the engines with a deafening roar, above which are heard the hoarse commands of the captain as he grinds in his gears. Then you realize that the thing is actually moving, that the bosses on the belt have managed to find a grip on the slime - and presently you come to the brink of what appears, to your exaggerated sense of perception, a bottomless chasm, with distant steep banks on the farther side that look unattainable and insurmountable. It is an old German trench which the rains have worn and widened. You brace yourself, you grip desperately a pair of brass handles in front of you, while leviathan hesitates, seems to sit up on his haunches, and then gently buries his nose in the pasty clay and paws his way upward into the field beyond. It was like sitting in a huge rocking-chair. That we might have had a bump, and a bone-breaking one, I was informed after I had left the scene of the adventure. It all depends upon the skill of the driver. The monsters are not as tractable as they seem.

That field in which the tanks manoeuvre is characteristic of the whole of this district of levelled villages and vanished woods. Imagine a continuous clay vacant lot in one of our Middle Western cities on the rainiest day you can recall; and further imagine, on this limitless lot, a network of narrow-gauge tracks and wagon roads, a scattering of contractors' shanties, and you will have some idea of the daily life and surroundings of one of oar American engineer regiments, which is running a railroad behind the British front. Yet one has only to see these men and talk with them to be convinced of the truth that human happiness and even human health thanks to modern science - are not dependent upon an existence in a Garden of Eden. I do not mean exactly that these men would choose to spend the rest of their existences in this waste, but they are happy in the consciousness of a job well done. It was really inspiring to encounter here the familiar conductors and brakemen, engineers and firemen, who had voluntarily, and for an ideal, left their homes in a remote and peaceful republic three thousand miles away, to find contentment and a new vitality, a wider vision, in the difficult and dangerous task they were performing. They were frequently under fire - when they brought back the wounded or fetched car-loads of munitions to the great guns on the ridiculous little trains of flat cars with open-work wheels, which they named - with American humour - the Federal Express and the Twentieth Century Limited. And their officers were equally happy. Their colonel, of our regular Army Engineer Corps, was one of those broad-shouldered six-footers who, when they walk the streets of Paris, compel pedestrians to turn admiringly and give one a new pride in the manhood of our nation. Hospitably he drew us out of the wind and rain into his little hut, and sat us down beside the stove, cheerfully informing us that, only the night before, the gale had blown his door in, and his roof had started for the German lines. In a neighbouring hut, reached by a duck board, we had lunch with him and his officers baked beans and pickles, cakes and maple syrup. The American food, the American jokes and voices in that environment seemed strange indeed! But as we smoked and chatted about the friends we had in common, about political events at home and the changes that were taking place there, it seemed as if we were in America once more. The English officer listened and smiled in sympathy, and he remarked, after our reluctant departure, that America was an extraordinary land.

He directed our chauffeur to Bapaume, across that

wilderness which the Germans had so wantonly made in their retreat to the Hindenburg line. Nothing could have been more dismal than our slow progress in the steady rain, through the deserted streets of this town. Home after home had been blasted - their intimate yet harrowing interiors were revealed. The shops and cafes, which had been thoroughly looted, had their walls blown out, but in many cases the signs of the vanished and homeless proprietors still hung above the doors. I wondered how we should feel in New England if such an outrage had been done to Boston, for instance, or little Concord! The church, the great cathedral on its terrace, the bishop's house, all dynamited, all cold and wet and filthy ruins! It was dismal, indeed, but scarcely more dismal than that which followed; for at Bapaume we were on the edge of the battle-field of the Somme. And I chanced to remember that the name had first been indelibly impressed on my consciousness at a comfortable breakfast-table at home, where I sat looking out on a bright New England garden. In the headlines and columns of my morning newspaper I had read again and again, during the summer of 1916, of Thiepval and La Boisselle, of Fricourt and Mametz and the Bois des Trones. Then they had had a sinister but remote significance; now I was to see them, or what was left of them!

As an appropriate and characteristic setting for the tragedy which had happened here, the indigo afternoon could not have been better chosen. Description fails to do justice to the abomination of desolation of that vast battle-field in the rain, and the imagination, refuses to reconstruct the scene of peace - the chateaux and happy villages, the forests and pastures, that flourished here so brief a time ago. In my fancy the long, low swells of land, like those of some dreary sea, were for the moment the subsiding waves of the cataclysm that had rolled here and extinguished all life. Beside the road only the blood-red soil betrayed the sites of powdered villages; and through it, in every direction, trenches had been cut. Between the trenches the earth was torn and tortured, as though some sudden fossilizing process, in its moment of supreme agony, had fixed it thus. On the hummocks were graves, graves marked by wooden crosses, others by broken rifles thrust in the ground. Shattered gun-carriages lay in the ditches, modern cannon that had cost priceless hours of skilled labour; and once we were confronted by one of those monsters, wounded to the death, I had seen that morning. The sight of this huge, helpless thing oddly recalled the emotions I had felt, as a child, when contemplating dead elephants in a battle picture of the army of a Persian king.

Presently, like the peak of some submerged land, we saw lifted out of that rolling waste the "Butt" of Warlencourt - the burial-mound of this modern Marathon. It is honeycombed with dugouts in which the Germans who clung to it found their graves, while the victorious British army swept around it toward Bapaume. Everywhere along that road, which runs like an arrow across the battle-field to Albert, were graves. Repetition seems the only method of giving an adequate impression of their numbers; and near what was once the village of Pozieres was the biggest grave of all, a crater fifty feet deep and a hundred feet across. Seven months the British sappers had toiled far below in the chalk, digging the passage and chamber; and one summer dawn, like some tropical volcano, it had burst directly under the German trench. Long we stood on the slippery edge of it, gazing down at the tangled wire and litter of battle that strewed the bottom, while the rain fell pitilessly. Just such rain, said my officerguide, as had drenched this country through the long winter months of preparation. "We never got dry," he told me; and added with a smile, in answer to my query: "Perhaps that was the reason we never caught colds."

When we entered Albert, the starting point of the British advance, there was just light enough to see the statue of the Virgin leaning far above us over the street. The church-tower on which it had once stood erect had been struck by a German shell, but its steel rod had bent and not broken. Local superstition declares that when the Virgin of Albert falls the war will be ended.

IV

I come home impressed with the fact that Britain has
learned more from this war than any other nation, and
will probably gain more by that knowledge. We are all
wanting, of course, to know what we shall get out of it,
since it was forced upon us; and of course the only
gain worth considering - as many of those to whom its
coming has brought home the first glimmerings of
social science are beginning to see - is precisely a
newly acquired vision of the art of self-government. It
has been unfortunately necessary - or perhaps
fortunately necessary - for the great democracies to
turn their energies and resources and the inventive
ingenuity of their citizens to the organization of armies
and indeed of entire populations to the purpose of
killing enough Germans to remove democracy's
exterior menace. The price we pay in human life is
appallingly unfortunate. But the necessity for national
organization socializes the nation capable of it; or, to
put the matter more truly, if the socializing process had
anticipated the war - as it had in Great Britain - the
ability to complete it under stress is the test of a
democratic nation; and hence the test of democracy,
since the socializing process becomes international.
Britain has stood the test, even from the old-fashioned
militarist point of view, since it is apparent that no
democracy can wage a sustained great war unless it is
socialized. After the war she will probably lead all
other countries in a sane and scientific liberalization.
The encouraging fact is that not in spite of her
liberalism, but because of it, she has met military
Germany on her own ground and, to use a vigorous
expression, gone her one better. In 1914, as armies go

today, the British Army was a mere handful of men whose officers belonged to a military caste. Brave men and brave officers, indeed! But at present it is a war organization of an excellence which the Germans never surpassed. I have no space to enter into a description of the amazing system, of the network of arteries converging at the channel ports and spreading out until it feeds and clothes every man of those millions, furnishes him with newspapers and tobacco, and gives him the greatest contentment compatible with the conditions under which he has to live. The number of shells flung at the enemy is only limited by the lives of the guns that fire them. I should like to tell with what swiftness, under the stress of battle, the wounded are hurried back to the coast and even to England itself. I may not state the thousands carried on leave every day across the channel and back again - in spite of submarines. But I went one day through Saint Omer, with its beautiful church and little blue chateau, past the rest-camps of the big regiments of guards to a seaport on th downs, formerly a quiet little French town, transformed now into an ordered Babel. The term is paradoxical, but I let it stand. English, Irish, and Scotch from the British Isles and the ends of the earth mingle there with Indians, Egyptians, and the chattering Mongolians in queer fur caps who work in the bakeries.

I went through one of these bakeries, almost as large as an automobile factory, fragrant with the aroma of two hundred thousand loaves of bread. This bakery alone sends every day to the trenches two hundred thousand loaves made from the wheat of western Canada! Of all sights to be seen in this place, however, the reclamation "plant" is the most wonderful. It covers acres. Everything which is broken in war, from a pair of officer's field-glasses to a nine-inch howitzer carriage is mended here - if it can be mended. Here, when a battle-field is cleared, every article that can possibly be used again is brought; and the manager pointed with pride to the furnaces in his power-house, which formerly burned coal and now are fed with refuse - broken wheels of gun-carriages, sawdust, and even old shoes. Hundreds of French girls and even German prisoners are resoling and patching shoes with the aid of American machinery, and even the uppers of such as are otherwise hopeless are cut in spirals into laces. Tunics, breeches, and overcoats are mended by tailors; rusty camp cookers are retinned, and in the foundries the precious scraps of cast iron are melted into braziers to keep Tommy in the trenches warm. In the machine-shops the injured guns and cannon are repaired. German prisoners are working there, too. At a distance, in their homely grey tunics, with their bullet-shaped heads close-cropped and the hairs standing out like the needles of a cylinder of a music-box, they had the appearance of hard citizens who had become rather sullen convicts. Some wore spectacles. A closer view revealed that most of them were contented, and some actually cheerful. None, indeed, seemed more cheerful than a recently captured group I saw later, who were actually building the barbed-wire fence that was to confine them.

My last visit in this town was to the tiny but on a "corner lot," in which the Duchess of Sutherland has lived now for some years. As we had tea she told me she was going on a fortnight's leave to England; and no Tommy in the trenches could have been more excited over the prospect. Her own hospital, which occupies the rest of the lot, is one of those marvels which individual initiative and a strong social sense such as hers has produced in this war. Special enterprise was required to save such desperate cases as are made a specialty of here, and all that medical and surgical science can do has been concentrated, with extraordinary success, on the shattered men who are brought to her wards. That most of the horrible fractures I saw are healed, and healed quickly - thanks largely to the drainage system of our own Doctor Carrel - is not the least of the wonders of the remarkable times in which we live.

The next day, Sunday, I left for Paris, bidding farewell regretfully to the last of my British-officer hosts. He seemed like an old, old friend - though I had known him but a few days. I can see him now as he waved me a good-bye from the platform in his Glengarry cap and short tunic and plaid trousers. He is the owner of a castle and some seventy square miles of land in Scotland alone. For the comfort of his nation's guests, he toils like a hired courier.

www.ingramcontent.com/pod-product-compliance
Lightning Source LLC
Chambersburg PA
CBHW032025040426

42448CB00006B/730